THE LIFE OF THE PARTY IS HARDER TO FIND UNTIL YOU'RE THE LAST ONE AROUND

THE LIFE OF THE PARTY IS HARDER TO FIND UNTIL YOU'RE THE LAST ONE AROUND

ADRIAN SOBOL

Mal
Arkey Books
Denver

©Adrian Sobol 2020

Published by Malarkey Books

PO Box 19713
Denver, CO 80219

www.malarkeybooks.com
@MalarkeyBooks

ISBN: 978-0-9981710-6-7

Cover design by Andrew Sobol
andrewsobol.com

Contents

11. The Bad News
12. The Emaciation Contest
13. Blackout Painting
14. The New Cosmos
16. There's No More Abstract Mode of Expressionist Art Than Dreams
19. Everyone Here Takes Everything So Seriously All the Time
20. Love Poem to You or No One in Particular
21. I Have This Joke I've Been Working On
22. I Have This Joke I've Been Working On
23. Halfway Through *Sixteen Candles*
24. Interior Design
25. Goldbluming
26. How to Leave a Party
35. Self-Portrait (After Buying a Top Chef 5-Piece Knife Set)
36. Special Delivery (Self-Portrait with Sexual Situations)
37. Other Updates from your Network
38. Octopus Nigiri
39. This is Hardcore
40. Garbage Poetry
42. Self-Portrait After *Self-Portrait in a Convex Mirror* by John Ashbery via *Self-Portrait in a Convex Mirror* by Parmigianino
43. "I Love to Watch Children Dying"
44. The Envoy
46. McConaughey Haiku (Just Keep Livin')
47. Mediocrity Blues
48. I Have This Joke I've Been Working On
50. Hey, That's No Way to Say Goodbye
53. The Last One Around
54. Tonguework (a second language)
55. To Those Dying to Get Out

57. Demonology (Aubade c. 2007)
59. There Was a War On
67. The Museum of Everyday Life*

"I do all these awful things—but don't you really think I'm awfully nice?"

— Elizabeth Bishop

The Bad News

I am given the bad news. I ring every number I can think of. If anyone ever picks up, if a voice arrives on the other end of the line, I will have to tell them the bad news. Then I will have no news. We will listen to each other breathing, nothing but the bad news between us. We will not speak for a long time. I begin to picture what this other person will look like, what their hands will do, the kinds of clothes they buy but never wear. This happens to me all the time. I have a closet full of shirts with no occasion. *Tonight is the night,* I think, *when the bad news will find someone.* I imagine what it will feel like, finally telling someone this & how just in the telling I will be free, how all the blood I have kept secret for so long will finally come to follow you home.

The Emaciation Contest
for Eric

My friend and I compete to see who can get skinny first. To see whose ribs will round off most like the bodies of shitty boys on New England beaches. I tell him, *I just had a piece of toast to eat today.* He says, *Yeah? I just had a cigarette.* I toss the toast from my house. He thinks about some crumbs at the bottom of a drawer. I tell him *I haven't eaten for three days.* He says, *I've been keeping stones in my mouth.* I say, *I starved the population of a small European city through a series of calculated trade sanctions*—which wins me the contest, but causes the people I love to whisper about me. The people I love begin to gather in rooms I'm not allowed into. The people I love say I have grown up to become terrifically horrible. Still, after all they have done, they continue to be the people I love.

Blackout Painting

I've felt this before / this carpeting / saw it spill / came to / in a crowd / watching / you are all such pleasing to look at people / in tonight's production / the part of this barren landscape / will be played by / a disembodied voice / listen / to it imitate / our blood's murmur / I want to speak to you / about how / I want to speak to you / you should know / what I'm capable of / I can fall / asleep through / the length of our conversations / not miss a thing / you like to yell / into a black sky / fill it up / with our frailty / we should not argue / instead / we should / stare / into each other's faces / until one / or both / of us crumble / while the planet / shoves us / through what's left of it

The New Cosmos

When the earth stops its spin
& hurls us from its cities

I could see us together
shoveled through the new cosmos

the new cosmos would look handsome on you
that emptiness would look good on anyone

the way most vacant expressions do
if only Elton wrote

some song for this occasion
I'd run up the volume

let it curdle yr hearing
see where that left us

I'm thinking Ottawa
but that's purely coincidental

we could live out our last days
in a motel room

dress in so many layers
we aren't able to move

the sun'll burn out one day
I don't want to be cold

it's been exhausting I mean
expensive I mean I love you but

until someone offers me yr photograph
how will I know the difference

between what I've kept
& what I haven't discarded

There's No More Abstract Mode
of Expressionist Art Than Dreams
or Lines You Would Have Excerpted From Our Interview
Had We Met on a Train to Talk
About My Forthcoming Novel:
a poem in three acts

I.

I confess nothing when caught alive
& once I even lived

in a lighthouse where
every other weekend

I held house
shows   house parties

& the most extravagant
shipwrecks you've ever seen

II.

In my new part-time job being mistaken
for other people   I've learned
there's no money in it
        little recourse against

promotion
plus a few things about how to behave

    I have attempted to catalogue
my every sin   I've given

out a 1-800 number

to call for updates
on my latest spree
    a must-try
service   the papers of record announced

    now (after years of this) I'm told I should try to improve
    as if every trainwreck is not already sincere

    I think about exercise
nothing too long or too strenuous

I just want to look
    like evening has come to barrel over me

III.

To make myself useful
        I have to turn into something else
placid
is one way to behave
        as a lake   out in the country

        barely
noticed but still there

I put a finger through
        the hole in my shirt
                then my arm
then by noon my whole body is lost to it

                how long
will this day go on before it has tired of itself

we have a right to be
tired   bored
        I put on a smile to try something
new

        it's only okay
        so far   art for

        art's sake upsets everyone

                it's the most radical form
                      of love   I know

Everyone Here Takes Everything So Seriously All the Time

Everyone here takes everything
so seriously all the time

look at the way they carry
their groceries
so seriously

look at the way they worry

were there not
parties we meant
to have?

were there not
friends who leapt
from doorways

ready to embrace us?

every time I recall their names
I think of the trouble
we used to build together

like model airplanes
so precise in scale
so detailed & miniature

one could mistake them for the real thing

Love Poem to You or No One in Particular

I walked over   with a mirror for a view
I walked over   with a hardwood floor

                  the housesized
                  capacity of my love

I may have dressed for the throat

but we took to the street taller
than evening

when we're this elegant
         we're not going to die

I could promise you this

I could promise us anything

it's why these words
were written to you

         or someone else who finds them

what you find
you will repeat indefinitely

what you repeat will reveal itself

to be yours

I Have This Joke I've Been Working On

"and God has many other surprises, like
When the man you fear most marries your mother"
  – John Berryman

about when I was younger
& Catholic & wanted
in light of vestments in
sight of clothwork & collar
to be a priest

I don't mean at all to bother
with why not

the joke it starts—it starts:
—there's this old saying—you can
take the prayer
     out of the boy
     but

I'm sorry   my hair's fucked
on earth as it is
     in heaven

I Have This Joke I've Been Working On

about a true crime
podcast

where every
episode

I hear myself
become

the victim
begging

to be saved before
the ad break

my meal kit
already on the way

Halfway Through *Sixteen Candles*

I realize it's *Pretty in Pink*
& halfway through I think
that dog asleep with Molly Ringwald
is dead & John Hughes is dead
& Jon Cryer will die though
not near as spectacularly
as we plan on going ourselves
what with the orchestra
pre-booked & a parade of craftsmen
ready to suture together our effigies
to look happier than we ever were
but it's not worth considering
in this spiraling airplane
the captain out of breath
the flight attendant half-
conscious near the beverage cart
someone left the lavatory
door unlatched so close to closing
if somebody would just reach out
when I recline against the sky
I won't sing "Try a Little Tenderness"
I'll divide my attention
b/w "These Arms of Mine"
& some saccharine K-pop number
I don't know the words to
        I'll just mouth something beautiful
        & maybe you will believe me

Interior Design

I keep my ghosts by the window
now they're drapes

Goldbluming

the floor made love to a
a broken cheek bone

a left   a left hook
the greatest suckerpunch
        in all of christendom

what's a   a Polish boy to do
but marvel &
spiral out poolside

rattle the clay
knot the iambic

& catalog the isthmus of
yr marbled laugh

How to Leave a Party

1.

I've been ghosting
since the first

grave

2.

I found this unopened
instructional videotape
on how to do some pretty
killer karate moves

If this is how we fall
in love   so be it

I'm ready
to be kicked
in the face
with a beam of light

3.

The gnostics had a word
for every word
describing our universe's
constant state

of sexual arousal

it appears on a list
of new exhibits
at the Museum
of Everyday Life®

4.

I have a vast network now
I know people in Cincinnati
why the dead grass grows in their lawns

I once had a kiss
so bad I kept coming
back to it
drove half the country down
some backshit road
not on any map to have it

put new cracks in my teeth

5.

My doctor tells me to have a goal
to be limber

I'm trying to touch my toes
in the future
I'm told
there will be dancing

yes, a little dancing
just enough
to lift up the sky

6.

A man on a tightrope has died
but not like you might expect

in his pocket
he had a new kind of poem

it's the first of its kind
the first with feathers
the first with hollow bones
you're thinking bird

don't

7.

Open threat: I'll sing "Hallelujah"
at karaoke

I'll sing the lost verses too
forgive me, Leonard

you were not meant
in my palm
to be a weapon

8.

I hold a knife
the music it plays across
      the seafloor is beautiful

I love its song

I've learned almost half the words

when I'm done you can bury me

I want to see what's underneath
you all the time

9.

Listen, we have two instincts: killer & basic
dress appropriately
        take account of yr limbs
                where you leave them
each night
        in the next room
as feathers rain around yr bed
an unspeakable horror washes its feet

10.

I want to tell you
about the curtain
I've cut eyeholes into & stood
behind

I was never a painter
but I could tell you were out
of proportion

from this angle

the floor doesn't appear
to be flooding

this isn't important
but the coffee table
        has floated away

11.

I grow
bored

I construct
an elaborate social experiment

I pretend to be one whole person

I don't tell anyone
no one knows

I stand in the rain & think
what if this were blood
I look up to see

today, it is

"*Monday*
Me.

Tuesday
Me.

Wednesday
Me.

Thursday
Me."
— Witold Gombrowicz

Self-Portrait (After Buying a Top Chef 5-Piece Knife Set)

Found in last night's quiet I was excited. I thought I finally heard my inner voice for the first time, or maybe Spicer whispering a poem on horseback from within. It was just my neighbors arguing. Dear neighbors, the wall isn't thick enough. Should we discuss it over dinner? I like my food thick enough so I feel it crack over the lull behind my eyes. I can't sit in silence without an encroach of panic or at least irony. I sleep at bare minimum to two sources of white noise. I buy things to put myself at a distance from myself & I like my things in multitudes to smother what's left of me out of the room. I've been talking to myself. More as a practice of intimacy than prayer. Okay, I'll be honest. There is no sound in space b/c there is no sound inside a vacuum. That's what terrifies me. When I said to Steve once *I'm dead inside,* Steve said to me *I'm dead inside & out.*

SPECIAL DELIVERY (SELF-PORTRAIT WITH SEXUAL SITUATIONS)

I could answer the door in a towel, if the towel did not imply that I have nothing to do. The public should look at me as if I'm busy. As if I have a reason to split the day open. If my hair is not right-angled, not dry, the doorknob will not demand enough to be turned. When the postman arrives, he wicks away the light from the blinds. I wonder what he thinks of the heft of my routine packages. He rarely discloses himself. Plus he never bothers to flirt. It's not an invitation. An invitation asks you to dress for the occasion. If only I had a robe to wear. Then even the night could be sutured closed with purpose. These days, I only get out of bed b/c I can't fall back asleep. I only get out of the shower b/c the water has gone cold. I only come to the door if a knock has come, like a thicket, unannounced.

Other Updates from your Network

after their last major email about "careerism"
how we should take to mending daylight
back into our wardrobe, maybe I'm ready to pester
the ash around me into something useful
not like a poem, more like a version of me
that's willing to improve—it's five after midnight
my mouth worn down in the small print
promise to unsubscribe every further update
from LinkedIn, yes, where the dressed go to chatter
& tell us we've got to be pliable, goal-oriented
I tell the recruiter my skillset is limited
but that lately I've taken to driving at night
with my eyes closed, meeting each intersection head-on
lips pressed into the air, ready to kiss the wheel

Octopus Nigiri

In back, I still keep a binder of photos of every animal I've ever eaten. The studies are inconclusive. There's eel or there's octopus & which one will put me in a better mood. I can ask a clouded room whether three-dimensional thinking, of which I'm told the octopus is capable, will provide a more satisfying meal. Last night not even a whim could make request of me. I just stood there, aching. Much of the earth works this way: the handsome women in the corner, the nearly-handsome men named Richard. Even the ashen conduction of memory is all but arbitrary. To think I once dreamt an ex wearing drapes as a dress. The party could barely contain itself. The valet's dog had to be hospitalized. Then in my inhale: reservations. What does it mean that I retire & avoid eye contact even in the dream? I can only aspire to demand—that classic fetter. I can only aspire to create problems I will myself not to solve.

This is Hardcore

so forgive me
I'm writing
to let you know

I've taken
the batteries

from the smoke
detector

to begin living

dangerously

Garbage Poetry

I like garbage poetry
I like flycrusted, offal poetry
I like dead, stuffed & waterlogged poetry
I like garbage poetry for its plastic bags
I like garbage poetry for its rotten fruit
its heels of stale bread
its rancid chicken not good enough to eat
as pink & gray as 23rd Avenue
in July alive with kids
on their bikes at our backs screaming
I like garbage poetry
dripping as it leaves on the way out the door
ready to perch
naked on curbs
asleep, slumping in the sun
on beaches & branches
& around the mouths of fish
inside a carcass
picked open by hungry gulls
I like garbage poetry
I like how it lingers
& says nothing
I like the earnest decay
of a rat-king thought
the gristled mass
of our undone lines
I like garbage poetry
for that matter
I like garbage men
I like garbage poetry for the same reason
I love garbage men
who lift me out the trash & toss me
into a larger pile of trash

garbage men will come over
once a week
garbage men will thrust
me into the earth
forgotten, compact
sacked into a landfill in Illinois
where each winter
fat snows cover us
where each winter
the teens go snowboarding
until one falls & then another
& another
& another
& another hard enough
to slip
a bone through skin
a bone through muscle
a bone through blood we point to
wiped across the powder
like some whisper
we overheard & passed on
they tell us go home
they tell us the park is closed
we finish our beer in the car
pour out the dregs to bless
those ghosts underneath
who speak less & less
their every desire weighed
against the language to convey it

Self-Portrait After *Self-Portrait in a Convex Mirror* by John Ashbery via *Self-Portrait in a Convex Mirror* by Parmigianino

>"*Him too we can sacrifice*
>*To the end progress, for we must, we must be moving on.*"
>— John Ashbery

I don't want to be "in a tradition." I want to be the one that wipes it out. The last stand, the final run on an equation that unbalances the effort. It's too simple to put ourselves into something. It's pulling out— that's the trouble. I had a dream, yes, about us & (this part is true) an anthology of men too old to be enjoyed anymore except in a joke or a telephone call. I titled the book THE EXPENDABLES because when I think of the poem "The One Thing That Can Save America" I think *John Rambo*. The rest you can map yourself. Listen, you're no longer men, but ideas. & ideas must be devoured by attrition—really, the only way to make love anymore—when this temple contrives itself into some fabulous ruin we can ignore, let them know I gave the thing a kick, & then it toppled down on me these oblations of some fine, ecstatic fortune.

"I Love to Watch Children Dying"

wrote Mayakovsky in "A Few Words About Myself." Was this a joke? It gets a laugh. Alone in my living room, I am not an insignificant part of it. *You all just clapped for a dead baby*, a comedian tells his audience, much later. Look, I want the force of a joke—it amounts to a glove anyway. I want to can it. Keep it in my root cellar for some common emergency, like a Cat 5 hurricane or a boring halftime show. But this is a poem & poetry only allows itself the serious babies (b/c poets are cruel). You know the kind I mean. The kinds of babies who, when the geese start to march into town, put on a daycare rendition of *Cabaret*. The kinds of babies who wear powder blue bowties, who have tasteful tattoos, who tote around opinions about the latest *New York Times* editorial. The kinds of babies who, god forbid, want one day to become academics. When you start to look, you can see them everywhere. In their tiny town cars. In their opera furs. You can feel them in your arms, fidgeting. They stare into the eyes of their mothers, or their fathers, & announce: *How drab, a polemic. I'll go put on my hat.*

The Envoy

I wake up every afternoon trying
not to be afraid

an American flag slipped through
      the hole in my Polish tongue
      I can't speak

a little ground down from submarine panic
      I can't walk

into a school without worrying
someone's weapon is going to make us news today

I can't even begin

to grieve

there's talk this country
      might have to

      bomb somebody
      soon

      I'll be willing

            to send
a volunteer

some friends

against my reservations
have children now

so yes of course I'm jealous

when I told Adam *I want to be the one everyone has to protect from the world*

I meant it

McConaughey Haiku (Just Keep Livin')

Remember to
breathe & eat alright
alright   alright

Mediocrity Blues

It's okay to feel accidental. Anecdotal evidence suggests we barely belong in the lives we make. We may all be better off in Boca! It's in the checkout magazine's interest to make you wait & consider options: the difference between content, contentment, & continent—which one, you think, is big enough for you? Sanctity occurs ounce on precious ounce (that sliced ham, sugar) while a city's constant hum makes up for our lack of assurance. How does that song go? Nothing gets better, does it, baby? Even in my lesser fantasies, my image hasn't been printed by *Us Weekly*—tabloids don't bother to meet me halfway. Hillary Clinton looks wrung. My cashier, tired & wrung. To say nothing of the rest of the crowd. Carts & figures with loose wheels, I feel you. It might be assumed, you know I've heard it before, repeated by those with expensive spiritual advisors that the tone of one's surroundings originates from within. Look at the sheer defeat that must faucet out of me. If this were a play, would a mother turn to her daughter to say in a hushed tongue, a finger sweet with air: *Don't look! This is when Adrian enters with his wallet out & poetry holstered*—a helm provided by a gym class orchestra, sweating, conducted in the pit? No! Of course not. There's yr problem, poet: you have the costume down but no horns to play you out.

I Have This Joke I've Been Working On
for Héctor

about how I can count
on one hand

a list of what
I'm grateful for

it's arbitrary
which is my way

of saying *Honest*

after hearing it
Héctor says

Oh

his way
of saying

Oh

you're fucked

I want to bail
this bar scene

but Héctor buys me a beer
asks me to stay

& that's what it takes

before I go
parade into the ocean

I tell him

Sing "Smooth" at karaoke

it's the closest I've come to thank you

Hey, That's No Way to Say Goodbye

When I stand on the edge
of a beach

the water always looks
like it has come

all this way
just to greet me

The Last One Around

You won't bother to look up
let sleep run down yr arms
back into the brush of a sweater
I want to call
ask how you'd like to be doing
not how you are
                      a car honks
at the light   my old shirt
broken under all those
train bells & spokes outside—

Do you notice how Chicago keeps its pace
without us? Our interior lives lacking
no good rooms to hide
our headaches in—
        how are we to stay busy?
You are the kind of person who'd say

        I sometimes manage
        to think of you fondly.

which I love b/c it's the only
honest thing worth telling anybody
        after a party
        we used to slur glances
our conversation drowsy
they were—our mouths—not quite
        as thirsty
        as the dog
at our ankles
allowing itself that beg
we've long learned
to ignore in ourselves

Tonguework (a second language)

It happens slowly the fester
of yr nightcap starts in

behind the fingernails a little
fly twisting its legs behind yr eyes

it's like this the crook of a neck
in yr palm set against the clockhand

of skin
count the pulses
        the shimmer

you have to cut one vein to see
you close yr eyes instead

let the tongue work like a knife
& play guessing games

in a field the flowers linger
where you press yr hand

into the earth   the earth is warm
enough to crawl into
              a body
      you won't dream of
anything less than the ghost of yr desire
once you open   yr mouth

To Those Dying to Get Out
   for Caroline

I promised
you this poem
but I'm tired
I have given up
looking for beauty
in the bricklight
of a hot house afternoon
the news reports
these countries
are coming
with bombs
reports
these climates
will collapse
reports that
while the water
in Oakland
is safe to drink
there is still lead
in the air
in the dirt
lead in our houses
lead left in our
clothes after the rain
what art
can you make
from that?
whatever
will come
eventually
to kill me
is already
on its way

quiet &
unforeseen
working tendrils
under the skin
against the air
you expect
its arrival
will be
unpleasant
not at all
like a poem
no not at all
like this

Demonology (Aubade c. 2007)

Into an empty church
we were swept
foxing our hands as far
as they could reach
thru the softness
of a stranger
imagine that
us sweatdrunk
our shoulders
in freefall un-
dressing against
a pew beside
the eyes
of our lord
our partners beside
the point I said
let's go make the best
of their disappointment
before we turned penitent
we were on our knees
we were righteous
we were protesting
Iraq & talking
factions
& intervention
& Israel
& Palestine
we were
in the mid-
west for the last time
people they have
been kind to me
open & ruminant

when I've asked
to be included
on their list of regrets
often I have
been invited in

There Was a War On

1.

Everybody thinks my obsession with dying is out
it's really the next big thing

let me explain

I often dream of the position
we will be found in
after we die

how we'll try
to look

like we knew
what we were doing

some nights
we're found
knotted in bed
two planets unwilling

to be thrust out alone

others it's me   in a car   going forty
& you   a hundred
miles off   years later

sometimes it's the sun
exhausted
gorged on light
that kills us

lately news of nuclear war
kicks me awake

2.

early this morning I mistake the cry
of an ambulance
        for an air raid siren

I catch my senses & celebrate
my good luck by staying
in bed a little later today

I sleep well
into the afternoon

here in my Oakland
in-law suite
the sun's knocked over & rusted out
by the fences next door

        do you remember
my second floor
apartment in Chicago?

the sunset came in like a fist
        full of flowers
cradling my roommate's cat to sleep

I did not hear the upstairs
neighbors come home but they were
fucking for the first time
in a month

I didn't turn up the radio

or pour honey on anyone

I didn't have to

I've spent enough time on the floor to know
how to be undressed
how to be cut open
by an unprompted compliment
I've been held up by less
than some slack cushion of rope

only recently have I become adequate
                 at things
I should have excelled
at years ago

now I look like
I'm trying too hard
like playing punk music
in my 30s or being earnest
       inside a poem for you

3.

what part of me will I gravel away
in the next ten years?
I won't remember poems
but here are half a dozen
jokes I've been writing

about the distance
between us

I'm sorry
they're not funny

newspapers
report   the rise
        & fall
        of the stock
        market

        what does it have to offer us
        to treat those ecstasies we're still recovering?

each morning I check
        my bank account

each morning
        I amount
        to a little more

so each evening I drive
        the value down

against my better judgment
I still watch the news
it's not good
it's not even getting better

one summer in Rogers Park I watched
soldiers in Baghdad glisten against humvees
        in the sand
there was a war on

I drank beer on the beach
        until
                I had to invent new ways
        to inherit the world

4.

I have this theory you get back
the hours of any blackout
in the form of dreams
            you drift through
              mine constantly
it's easy to fall into the past

            some days
     it isn't worth it
to go outside
the dogs howl
         the breeze makes it through the curtains

that's enough

weather
     doesn't change
         in Oakland

     I can't recall how long I've lived here
     when someone asks I say
     my knees hurt more

     & the birds still leave in the winter

     it's how we recognize the sky

you reveal *a man*
once texted me to say
the rain reminded him of me

I ask myself
     Did I say that? No,
     but so what?

what doesn't the rain return to us?

      when it taps at my window
          it's gentle

when the armies ready their missiles
    the rain will be at its worst
                still gentle

The Museum of Everyday Life®

What they call "self-indulgence" is actually a lack
of explicit framework. A bolster to keep up
a tricky economy. A river just wide enough
to call its crossing an unexpected vacation.
Convincing everyone every city isn't
Fort Lauderdale—that's the greatest trick
the devil ever pulled. In keeping with history,
here's a rabbit, its entrails read by a witch doctor,
who turns to you as one harbinger of death to
another with breaking news. The position
of prime minister will never be yours to resign.
Take it, open this package, but only if you enjoy
conditional phrases. Inside you'll find plans
for discreet & state-approved factory farming based
on the selected works of George Oppen. That Russian
Roulette scene you like in *The Deer Hunter* as the #4 reason
we can't forgive *Reindeer Games*. My exhibitionism's
still under contract. Most of what I have to say
was lifted off men's room walls & discarded
pizza boxes. That's where I got my catchphrase:
Hot & Ready! Here are the odds against you.
Vacancies upon request. Provided herein: a
freshly copied call sheet enumerating
the requests of Abernathy's renowned
Breakfast Choir™. As delightful oxymorons go,
how's about "best secondary
education." Though you have had a name

for years & are encouraged when strangers use
it in a sentence in yr vicinity it remains
a "working title." You asked for it
now go live in the evening. Or the evening's uniform
swatch. On the pillar, a sign in German you can't
read: *Industry Night This Way.*
An arrow underneath makes
itself clear. Have you read yr Marx,
yr Neruda? Enough to say *proletariat
of petals and bullets* without worrying
about how sincere you stand? Instability
makes for a nation of poets. Turning to what?
Turning again to what we don't understand
to tell us why we're once more in the
right. Find a road into true realism
through a dream populated by the types
of people who wish they were you.

                      Vaccines sourced
from a mother cow, lowing in the field.
I've been there. Spreading my ass to the sky.
It was my favorite pastime after cycling
became cornered by medicine. They call
off-season training, as if you're not getting
better when you perform yr job during
scheduled hours. Like the entire month of
means testing. I, poet, love to forget
passively a day overcome with
gray so slowly you barely notice until it's
there in front of you, asking for change,

its tail wagging against a tree,
chewing an inexact replica of the leaf you
imagine when I say over the phone
one afternoon to change the subject,
Think of a leaf. That one you know
the one, the one you haven't seen in years,
but it still plays in yr mind as the stand-in for foliage.

The New York Times® arrives
in a plain black suit one
could be inclined to call
"unintelligible." *Perfect*, you think
you see Jesus making
balloon animals on his porch again.
We all need a day job. I met a lot
of nice people through
making knives. Off the record: I'm still unsure of
what makes up indelible ink. Didn't
think to study it. Didn't think to ask
when I first mixed up carbon dating for
things to do in Denver® when you're dead.
You can look up the answer at any time,
but as is often the case with Google™, you somehow
never do. I find, though, when I ask
my phone, after I'm stricken awake in the middle
of & by some callous unknown,
What's that sound? Google™ provides
less conclusive answers than the man tied up
next door. I could have asked him
to stop kicking. Something has been

listening to me making out
again. Maybe it has horns. Maybe even
a pair of rollerskates but don't bet on it.
Me? I don't gamble. My kink is
commodity fetishism. My money wants
a more simple life. The days pile on.
Inside an early memory. Which Chumbawamba
song? It's hard to tell
what a dog is thinking when he isn't
in the room with you. Accept
the invitation. Skip the party.

You decide today you can't spell
"artisanal" w/o first having to spell
"art is anal." The same can be said of a word
like "buttonhole," which has a "butthole"
in clear view. No one fans away their
shame. I'm still trying to crack a great
joke without being at the end of
one. I can go no further. My
expeditions flagged at the summit. No
less than fewer than. Suppose for a
minute I want & ought to be serious.
That that is a notion that can hold.
Leaking, as they say in the mouth
of the Great White
North*——is *all* relative.
A boat, dangling in the reeds,
leaks, while its the creek that makes itself welcome.
Nature always wins, says the fence outgrown

by the seesaw. What isn't in
competition? Before oxygen
only a handful of not-so famous elements.

This was *the* year
for planes falling out of view from multiple
radar screens. This was the year
the ocean accrued an airline. Naturally. Does an
invading force ever think, *Maybe I'm coming
on too strong*? Go tell payroll. If my letter is in the mail
you should expect it. What wouldn't you call
un-inevitable? In Nantucket®, a birdcall is tantamount
to an estranged lover, curbside & drunk, pretending
to not want to sleep with you. In other words, not worth
the rejoinder. There ought to be
a law against it or at the very least
a circumcision. For comparison's
sake. Four out of five dentists
agree I'm more of an
anteater myself. Whereas outside
some car alarm patrols the blue
oven of dawn.

                    Needless
excess as its own privacy. You write
that down. You might even own it.
You're unsure of the current statutes
regarding—what was it again? A man about yr age
promptly thinks of you w/o learning
yr name. At certain angles, yes, you do

stop looking like yourself & gain
a kind of "deer in a fulsome prairie"
gaze. Which isn't to say beautiful but
I wouldn't draw the hangman's card against
a sailboat either. You must have played
that game. It was all we did
growing up in the Midwest®. We'd pick
up the phone & count to one hundred
if we were lucky. If we were
the phone would echo
the world back to us. *I've got
bad news*, it would say. For
sale: Anticipation™. *Are we in
a snuff film?* you ask, fingers through
my teenage hair. A*re we in
God's snuff film?* Too late
into four a.m. to even think
about what's sinister. It's perpetually
out of view. Squint. I dare you. Tears
mask what's coming behind those headlights. You
can discern the studio audience
shifting, discomfited, in their chairs.
O distinct carrier wave of comedy! You're
almost home. A woman across the hall laughs.
Maybe she doesn't mean it, but we have to hear.

Acknowledgements

I'd like to thank Steve, Rachel, Kolby, Héctor, Vanessa, Caroline, Adam and everyone who, back in Colorado, were such a source of inspiration and encouragement. Thanks to Ruth Ellen Kocher and Noah Eli Gordon for their patience and guidance. Enormous gratitude to Joshua Marie Wilkinson for showing me poetry could be a path.

Thanks to Jennifer Wortman and Alan Good for helping save this project and giving it a second chance when it was as good as dead.

Thank you to my parents, Artur and Teresa. Thanks, Andrew for the beautiful cover. And Melissa for everything.

Earlier versions of these poems have appeared in *Vagabond City*, *Hardly Doughnuts*, *Five Quarterly*, *Reality Beach*, *Window Cat Press*, and *No Assholes*.

The line "Most of what I have to say was lifted off men's room walls" is an interpolation of a lyric written by David Berman. The book's title belongs to the song "Dead Friends" by The Saps.

www.ingramcontent.com/pod-product-compliance
Lightning Source LLC
Chambersburg PA
CBHW030457010526
44118CB00011B/982